Through these beautiful personal devotions
Karen inspires readers to . . . . ays provide
to God . . . san Heim, co-editor, *Chicken Soup for
the Soul: Devotional Stories for Women*

Having known Karen for many years, I can attest
that her examples in *Becoming a Woman of Purpose*
are true and meaningful. When you go through
these for a month, your faith will be enlarged,
and your spiritual life will be lifted.

—Florence Littauer, author and speaker

BECOMING A
WOMAN OF PURPOSE

Becoming a
Woman of Purpose

Karen R. Kilby

Tate Publishing *& Enterprises*

Published by Tate Publishing & Enterprises, LLC
127 E. Trade Center Terrace | Mustang, Oklahoma 73064 USA
1.888.361.9473 | www.tatepublishing.com

Tate Publishing is committed to excellence in the publishing industry. The company reflects the philosophy established by the founders, based on Psalm 68:11,
"The Lord gave the word and great was the company of those who published it."

Book design copyright © 2011 by Tate Publishing, LLC. All rights reserved.
Cover design by Kellie Southerland
Interior design by Nathan Harmony
Author photo by Carolyn Prescott, Prescott Photography

Published in the United States of America

ISBN: 978-1-61739-933-6
1. Religion: Christian Life: Devotional
2. Religion: Christian Life: Women's Issues
11.01.07

DEDICATION

To my children, Kurt, Susan and Joe, Michael, Keith and Ceia, and to all thirteen of my beautiful grandchildren.

"Be very careful never to forget what you have seen God doing for you. May his miracles have a deep and permanent effect upon your lives. Tell your children and your grandchildren about the glorious miracles he did" (Deuteronomy 4:9).

ACKNOWLEDGMENTS

I want to thank my beloved husband, David; my beautiful "Butterfly Friend," Carol; and my devoted mentor, Erin, who had the vision for this book long before I even caught a glimpse of the dream.

Many thanks also to Janet Wood and all my sisters in Christ at First Presbyterian Church of Kingwood, Texas, for being my readers and encouragers in the beginning stages of the manuscript.

A special thank you to Florence and Marita Littauer of CLASServices, Inc., whose mentoring opened the door for several of my life experience stories to be published independently with Chicken Soup for the Soul series and other publications, giving me the confidence to believe in my writing.

And to Tate Publishing for making this dream come true, for believing it really was a great idea. Most of all, I am truly grateful to my loving heavenly Father for being the author of every life experience shared in these pages.

THE QUEST

You will find me when you seek me, if you
look for me in earnest.

Jeremiah 29:13

The search for fulfillment is a lifelong process
that begins and ends with God. My search began
as a young girl, often wondering, *Why was I born
in this time and place?* Surely, I thought, my ques-
tions would be answered when I met and married
Prince Charming. He would become my king, I
would be his queen, and we would live happily

ever after. Motherhood was another pursuit I thought would bring fulfillment, but after four children and trying to be the keeper of the castle, I found myself searching for my own identity. Many times I found myself thinking, *Is this all there is to life? There has to be more than this!*

Several times I found myself sharing my concerns with my close friend Marie as we met for coffee. The more I shared my unrest, the more Marie sensed my need to discover *God's* design for my life. We had never discussed spiritual things before, yet she realized I needed to establish a relationship with God through his son, Jesus, before I could even begin to know my reason for being. Stepping out of her comfort zone, Marie gave me a book called *Peace with God*, by Billy Graham. The title intrigued me.

As I began to read, I was astonished to discover Billy Graham knew so much about me, yet we had never met. He seemed to know all about the emptiness I was feeling inside and all the ways I was trying to fill it. Billy Graham continued to tell me the void in my life had actually been created by God so that I would recognize my need for him. As he shared verses from the Bible, one seemed to leap from the page. Jesus said, "My purpose is to give life in all its fullness" (John 10:10). Was this the answer I was looking for? Would I finally discover the reason for my existence? I sensed I had nothing to lose and everything to gain by believing this promise.

Upon accepting God's plan for my life, I began to experience a contentment I had never felt before. My role as a wife and mother took on new meaning, and none too soon. My king was about to abdicate the throne of our marriage. It was obvious that my previous discontent had infected our relationship. Yet I knew that God held the answer and this could be the beginning of discovering his purpose for both of us. Each day I asked God for his love for my husband, and each day he gave it. As David responded, we began to learn how to live happily ever after, God's way.

Oh how important it would be to have God's fortification for the battles ahead. When facing teenage rebellion, God gave us the ability to see this child with his eyes of unconditional love. When dealing with David's unemployment, God gave us hope by providing for our needs in miraculous ways. When coping with a family suicide, God gave us the peace that passes all understanding. When faced with a monumental financial crisis, God gave us the ability to trust him to lead us through it. When confronted with a substance abuse problem, God reminded us that love covers a multitude of faults.

Despite knowing that God had been there in every situation, I still questioned the reason. *What good is there in all of this? God, don't you care about your reputation, even if you don't care about ours?* Repeatedly his answer seemed to be, "It is not about your reputation or mine. It's about glorifying me in the battle. Whether I come to your rescue or not, it's about how high you hold my banner. My intent is to make you more like me."

More like him. More like the King of kings and Lord of lords. I had seen God do marvelous things in each of those situations, coming to our rescue over and over. Each time I was filled with amazement and gratitude for what he had done. But the process was not easy to live through.

Often it hurt, and I wanted to avoid the pain. What was his purpose in the pain?

The answer came in reading 2 Corinthians 1:3–4.

> What a wonderful God we have. He is the Father of our Lord Jesus Christ, the source of every mercy, and the one who so wonderfully comforts and strengthens us in our hardships and trials. And why does he do this? So that when others are troubled and needing our sympathy and encouragement, we can pass on to them this same help and comfort God has given us.

It is my prayer that as you take this thirty-one day journey with me, you too will discover an extraordinary God.

A Marriage Made
in Heaven

Wives, fit into your husband's plans for if
they refuse to listen when you talk to them
about the Lord, they will be won by your
respectful, pure behavior. Your godly lives
will speak to them better than any words.

1 Peter 3:1

We sat across the kitchen table from each other,
not quite knowing what to say. We had just come
from a counseling session with a pastor of a local

church. It was my hope that if anyone had the answer to saving our marriage, it would be God and this pastor could lead us to him. The pastor's advice was exactly what I expected. If we trusted God to be a part of our marriage, God would help us overcome our differences.

"Well," David said, "you are the one with the connection to God," as he got up from the table and left for work.

Connected to God. How good it felt to be connected to God. I wanted to be connected to David too. We had been married for ten years and had four beautiful children and a lovely home. Anyone looking at us from the outside would have thought we had it all together. The truth of the matter was we were on the verge of a separation. If it hadn't been for my friend Marie, I would not have known how to connect to God.

As I sat at the table contemplating what David had said, the thought came to me that I should call him at work and say, "I love you." Where in the world did that thought come from? God must certainly know I did not have those feelings at the moment. The thought persisted, and it was as if God was telling me he would provide what I needed at just the right time. So I made the call. David's response was, "You don't know how much I needed to hear that." When I hung up, I thought, *That was great*! Then it hit me. He'd be coming home at five! Then what? At that moment I felt God prodding me to meet him at the door with a hug and a kiss and again reminding me that he would give me what I needed at just the right time. And he did!

When I began to study the Bible, I learned the love passage that explained what God had been teaching me.

> Love is very patient and kind; never jealous or envious, never boastful or proud, never haughty, selfish or rude. Love does not demand its own way. It isn't irritable or touchy. It doesn't hold grudges and will hardly even notice when others do it wrong. It is never glad about injustice, but rejoices whenever truth wins out. If you love someone, you will be loyal to him no matter what the cost. You will always believe in him, always ex-

pect the best of him and always stand your
ground defending him.

1 Corinthians 13:4–7

I understood, perhaps for the first time, that it
wasn't what David could do for me but what God
could do inside my heart. That was such a different way of living and loving than what I had
ever experienced. I used to say, "Three strikes and
you are out!" Now I was given a choice of how I
could react and relate. I could choose to follow
God's unconditional love for David or my natural
instinct to be unforgiving and selfish.

David began to notice the changes in me were
real and responded to God's love himself. The
Bible says, "When someone becomes a Christian,
he becomes a brand new person inside. He's not
the same anymore. A new life has begun" (2
Corinthians 5:17). That's what happened to me
and to David.

Prayer

Thank you, Father, for your transforming, unconditional love that offers me a new beginning.

Discovery

Have you discovered God's transforming love for
your life?

New Adventures

Your words are a flashlight to light the path
ahead of me and keep me from stumbling.
Psalm 119:10

"Tom and I are moving our family to Florida, and we
want you and David to bring your family with us!"

I looked at June with astonishment. *Was she
crazy? Why on earth had they chosen us to move with
them? We were friends but not best friends.*

"Come on over Friday night. We'll play cards
and talk about it," she said.

David agreed. "That's the craziest idea I've ever heard!" But by Friday night, David had a plan. Why not take the pizza business from Michigan to Florida? Both David and Tom had bought a franchise from the owner and knew he just might go for the idea of expanding into another state. David and Tom realized this could be the opportunity they were looking for.

Naples, Florida, was the paradise our friends had chosen, as far south and as close to the beautiful white sandy beach as possible. Gainesville, Florida, would be the site of the first store, close to the University of Florida.

The owner of the franchise company agreed it was an opportunity for all of them. The papers were drawn up, and Florida became a pioneer state for David and Tom to conquer. Houses and businesses were put up for sale, and we headed south on our new adventure. Now we were all crazy, crazy about the idea of living in Naples, Florida!

A Realtor found our friends their beach home and a home with a pool for our family. Neither of us had seen our new homes until we pulled up with rental trucks stacked high with our possessions and station wagons loaded down with our kids. All we had to do was move our furniture into the tastefully decorated houses, leaving nothing for us to do but enjoy the beach and the pool with our families. We couldn't be happier.

Living in Florida was a dream come true for me as well as for June. I remembered my Florida vacations and thinking, *if I could only live here in paradise, I'd be happy.*

At that time, I did not realize that only God could really make me happy. Just a few months before the invitation had come for the move, God had become a vital part of my life.

I was excited about this new adventure taking place. Even though I had left behind newly developed Christian friendships in Michigan, I was confident that God would provide friendships for me here. I prayed for opportunities to make friends and to learn to study the Bible.

Our kids soon settled into the neighborhood, making their own friends. One day our son Michael ventured down the street. He had made a new friend with a boy just a few doors away. When I came to bring Michael home for dinner, I was invited into the house. Much to my delight, I noticed a Bible sitting on the desk. "Are you a Christian?" I exclaimed. "I'm a new Christian, and I want to learn how to study the Bible!" I soon discovered my neighbor had been praying for her own adventure, to have a neighborhood Bible study in her home, and was asking God to send the women to her. I became even more excited, realizing that God had strategically placed me where he knew I needed to be.

A couple of days later as I waited in the beauty shop to have my hair cut, a young woman noticed the title of the book I was reading and couldn't wait to come over to talk. "Are you a Christian?" she asked. "I'm a new Christian and just moved here from Ohio. Do you know how I can become involved in a Bible study?" I quickly gave her my new neighbor's address.

How awesome it was to see God bring us together one by one into a new adventure we could all share. In just a few weeks time, eight women, including June, met on a weekly basis to discover how God's Word would be relevant to our lives, an adventure that could last a lifetime.

Prayer

Thank you, Father, that when we study your Word we can know you better and learn how you want us to live. Thank you for the special friendships that we can share when we study your Word together.

Discovery

Are you discovering God's truth for your life by studying the Bible? If not, begin the adventure by getting involved in a Bible study at your church or through a friend.

Prayer Moves the Hands of God

Ask and you will receive, and your cup of
joy will overflow.

John 16:24

It was a beautiful morning. *The sun feels so good*,
I thought as I walked home from my neighborhood Bible study. *It isn't just the sunshine making
me feel so exuberant, so alive today. It's the excite-*

ment I feel when I'm with everyone studying your Word, Lord. How I wish David could feel it too.

David was very supportive of my newfound faith, continuing to reap the benefits of the positive changes taking place in me. Yet there seemed to be a hesitation to accept God's gift for himself.

Walking up the driveway to our home, I noticed David sitting out by the pool engrossed in reading. *What is he doing home so early? His appointment with the potential investor cannot be over this soon!* David looked up as I approached. "Home so soon? What happened?" I asked.

"The investor wasn't there when I went to meet him, so I decided to come back home and read the book you had recommended while I wait for his return phone call."

As I realized what was happening, I became delirious with joy! David was reading Pat Boone's book *A New Song*. I had just finished reading it. I had hoped and prayed that if David could read how God had worked through a financial situation for Pat Boone, perhaps he would also know God could do the same for him. I was not convinced that having a stranger invest in David's company was the best solution. But when would he find the time to read it before the appointment? Time was short, much too short for David to read the book before the scheduled meeting. It never occurred to me that God could rearrange David's calendar to give him the time he needed!

It took most of the day out by the pool for David to finish reading the book. The next morning as David was getting ready to leave for the rescheduled appointment, he turned to me with a smile and said, "Don't worry about this meeting today, Karen. I have given this situation over to God. I am trusting him to handle it along with every other situation in my life."

As David walked out the door, there was a new confidence evident in his demeanor. The same confidence was still on David's face when he returned, without the investor's money.

Prayer

Thank you, Father, that your timing is perfect!

Discovery

Did you know that all things are possible with God? Ask, so that your joy will be full!

The Ugly Duckling

Don't copy the behavior and customs of this
world but be a new and different person with
a fresh newness in all you do and think.

Romans 12:2

I could not believe my eyes! *This* was God's
answer to our prayers? The house was ugly! It
was gray and dark, inside and out. Tall pine trees
shaded the front of the house from the sun. The
backyard was a litter of foxholes and bunkers
resembling military engagements from the previ-

ous homeowner's boys. The center of attention from my kitchen window was a roofless greenhouse filled with plants securely anchored to the ground by roots penetrating the rusted tin cans. Inside, the bare floors and walls made the house look dingy and dull. I should have known the house was not picture perfect when David persuaded me to move, sight unseen, offering to paint and wallpaper. It was nothing I had imagined it would be, nothing like the house God had provided sight unseen in Naples.

The house fit the description of the ad we had placed in the paper for a four-bedroom home in the neighborhood where we wanted to live. I knew that God had met our family's need to find a home in Gainesville so David could manage the pizza store. *But why would God put us in a home that needed so much work?* Fixing up homes was what I used to enjoy. However, now that I was a new Christian, all I wanted to do was concentrate on learning about God.

Despite David's promise and effort to fix the house to my liking, I found myself becoming just as gray as I thought the house was. What a shock to look at myself in the mirror one morning and actually think my skin had turned gray! I realized I had to change the way I was thinking and accept God's gift exactly the way he had given it.

Christmas came. Instead of sending our normal newsletter with events of the family, we decided to share what we had discovered about the true meaning of celebrating Christmas. Our landlord and his new wife, Nancy, had moved to Hawaii for the year. In their card, I mentioned they were part of our story of how God had provided for our needs. A few months later I received a letter in return. It was from Nancy. She explained that when they had moved from Florida to Hawaii, Nancy had thought she was moving to paradise and that there she would find the happiness she was looking for with her new husband. It wasn't long before Nancy discovered her life was no different than it had been and she began to contemplate suicide.

When Nancy's daughter came to celebrate Christmas, she read the newsletter we had sent and bought her mother the book I had mentioned that had opened my eyes to God's truth: *Peace with God* by Billy Graham.

Nancy began to read the book, struggling through the pages even though she had three PhDs to her credit. One morning shortly after reading, while taking her shower, she found herself reflecting on all the Scripture verses she had memorized as a teen in hopes of winning Christian summer camp attendance with her church. Nancy remembered attending camp and having the opportunity to accompany the young youth director by playing the piano during the services, yet never responding to the powerful messages he had given as everyone else had. As the shower cleansed her body, Nancy felt God cleansing her heart. God was once again speaking to her through that same young man who was now, several years later, the author of *Peace with God*, Billy Graham. This time, Nancy responded.

As I read Nancy's letter, I realized God had given me that house for a reason that could not be seen on the surface. *This is not an ugly house anymore. It's the most beautiful home I've ever lived in.*

Prayer

Thank you, Father, for giving us your perspective on the circumstances of our lives. Help us to accept your gifts as they are and realize that blessings will follow.

Discovery

Has God put you in a place that you find hard to understand? Believe his Word that says, "The foolishness of God is wiser than the wisdom of man" (1 Corinthians 1:25).

Love Your Neighbor

You must love others as much as yourself.

Mark 12:31

We were excited about moving into our new home. The lease was up on the rental home, and now we had the opportunity to own a house large enough for our family of six, even having a guest room for company. As we settled in, we looked forward to getting acquainted with our new neighbors on the wooded cul-de-sac.

Our new next-door neighbor was a single working mom in her thirties, with teenage children close in age to ours. Gail was an attractive, well-dressed woman with a hat to match every outfit, her trademark that set her apart in the highly competitive real estate market in which she worked. Getting to know Gail was easy. We would often meet at the mailboxes at the end of our driveways or while working in our yards. From what Gail heard from the other neighbors, she thought we were a religious family and brought God into our conversations on several occasions.

One morning while visiting in our home, Gail commented, "I feel something different in your home. You know, as a Realtor, I am in many homes, and I don't sense in them what I feel here. I can feel love in every room in this house."

I was touched by her compliment of God's love being so evident.

As we continued to get better acquainted over the next few weeks, I sensed Gail did not have an intimate relationship with God. I prayed, "God, how can I introduce Gail to you?" His answer came with another question. "Why don't you roll up that talk you gave at the Christian Women's Club luncheon, tie it with a red ribbon and put it in her mailbox?" That sounded like a great idea to me, so I did.

The following day I found a smaller scroll tied with a red ribbon placed in my mailbox. As I slipped off the ribbon, I read Gail's message. "I was touched by what you have shared and have decided to accept God into my life. What's next?" Soon our mailboxes bulged with books being constantly passed back and forth as Gail eagerly absorbed as much as she could. As fast as Gail finished reading one book, I would give her another, prompting meaningful discussions of a daily walk with God. Our friendship deepened as we became tied together with his love.

A few years later, Gail moved away. Not long after, I heard of her untimely death and was saddened to know I had lost this special friend. As I mourned her loss, the refrain "blessed be the tie that binds our hearts in Christian love" reminded me that God was still the tie that would bind our hearts for all time. How glad I was that I had responded to God's perfect timing to love my neighbor with a scroll tied with his red ribbon of love.

Prayer

Thank you, Father, for helping me to love my neighbor enough to put aside any discomfort I may have in talking about you. Thank you for giving me opportunities to share your love with my neighbor, a friend or someone at work.

Discovery

Has God placed someone in your life that needs to hear of his love? Are you willing to share it?

Gone Fishin'

If you had faith even as small as a tiny mustard seed you could say to this mountain, "Move!" and it would go far away. Nothing would be impossible.

Matthew 17:20

"Hey, Mom! Where are you?" Kurt hollered, slamming the back door behind him.

What in the world is the problem? I wondered as I hurried to find out what was wrong.

"Nothing's wrong, Mom. Everything's just right! I've been invited to a fishing camp! The Gainey boys go every summer, and they want me to come too! All you have to do is call the camp. Call Mrs. Gainey to get the phone number. *Please*, Mom! It will be a blast," Kurt exclaimed, his dark brown eyes twinkling with excitement. "The camp is on an island up in the Florida Panhandle. You even have to take a raft from the mainland to get to the camp. Isn't that cool? It's a whole week of camping out and learning how to catch all kinds of fish!"

"When does it start?" I asked, smiling at my oldest son as he pushed his curly hair underneath his baseball cap.

"In a couple of weeks, so you have to call right away. They'll have room for me. Just call!"

I was touched by my twelve-year-old's optimism and moved by his enthusiasm. He hadn't fished much before, but I could tell he was anxious to learn. "Okay," I promised. "I'll call Mrs. Gainey for the phone number."

"Thanks, Mom," Kurt yelled as he ran back out the door to share his good news.

"I'd be glad to give you the phone number," Mrs. Gainey said that evening, "but I really think it's too late for the camp to have an opening for Kurt. The boys that attend go back year after year, even registering for the next year before they leave the camp. There is rarely a vacancy."

"Well," I replied with a sinking feeling, "I promised Kurt I would call. I'll have to try early tomorrow morning."

"Lord," I implored, dialing the number for the camp, "Kurt has his heart set on going to this camp with his new friends. He seems so sure that he will be able to go. I wish I had that much faith to believe he can. He'll be devastated if he can't. If it's possible, please let there be a vacancy."

With my fingers crossed and my heart in prayer, I voiced Kurt's request to the camp director. "Is there any way you would have room for my twelve-year old son who has his heart set on coming to your camp?"

"Mrs. Kilby," he said with astonishment, "you won't believe this! Just this very moment I hung up the phone from someone who had to cancel.

Otherwise, there would be no way that Kurt could come. Put your check in the mail, and he is in!"

Hanging up the phone, I became just as excited as Kurt over fishing and astounded that God was too! I couldn't wait to tell Kurt!

Prayer

Thank you, Father, that even faith as tiny as a mustard seed can move mountains, making room for a twelve-year-old boy.

Discovery

Do you hesitate to ask God for help when you think it's an impossible situation? Even the smallest of faiths can move a mountain!

FROM MOTHER-IN-LAW
TO MOTHER IN LOVE

I demand that you love each other as much
as I love you.

John 15:12

It had been a difficult relationship, almost non-existent. My mother-in-law's drinking problem
stood in the way of having a normal one.

As we began to raise our family, this became
more and more of a concern. However, now my

husband, David, was having a change of heart, telling me he wanted to offer his dad a job, of all things. He would fly back to his parents' home in Michigan, pack up their belongings and drive them to our home in Florida. And even worse, they would live with us for six weeks while the condo they had purchased was being renovated! What a turn of events! We had been relieved to have the distance between us when we moved to Florida five years before. What in the world had happened to change David's mind?

Ever since David had turned his life over to God, I had seen positive changes taking place. He was becoming more tenderhearted. It was evident in how David interacted with me and with the children, which I loved, but this decision was something I was finding very difficult to accept! How would I live with an alcoholic, even if only for six weeks? I knew David had made up his mind, so I prayed and prayed again in desperation. *I don't want to do this. Lord, help me to be willing! I'll open my home, but you will have to open my heart.*

When David's parents arrived, it was as though they sensed and respected my unspoken request.

Even though at times they were at odds with each other, they seemed to enjoy being with us. Gradually, we began to see changes taking place between them, especially changes in my mother-in-law. She had an aura of peace about her that had not been there before. She seemed to be more relaxed and enjoying life, greeting me each morning with a smile. We could actually enjoy each other's company, going to lunch together, shopping together, and planning meals together. As we visited, we became friends for the first time.

Soon, I learned the reason for the changes I saw, the result of a changed heart. Just before David had offered his dad a job, his mother had fallen and broken her hip. While recovering in the hospital, one of the nurses discovered she liked to read and gave her *The Hiding Place* by Corrie Ten Boom. As she read Corrie's book, my mother-in-law found her own hiding place as she realized and accepted God's love for herself.

A strong and loving friendship developed between us as we shared our God-centered common interests. She became not my mother-in-law but my Mother-in-love.

Prayer

Father, help me not to underestimate the power of your love. Help me to be willing to pass it on to others.

Discovery

Is there someone in your life who is difficult to love? Have you asked God for his love that covers a multitude of faults?

Seventy Times Seven?

If you are angry, don't sin by nursing your
grudge. Don't let the sun go down with you
still angry. Get over it quickly.

Ephesians 4:26

The shrill cry of the alarm woke me from an
uneasy sleep. Despite the softer greeting of the
morning songbirds and the promise of sunshine
glimmering through the curtains, I was reluctant
to get out of bed.

Duty calls, I muttered, knowing it was time to wake the kids for school. Making my way to the kitchen to start breakfast, I realized my disgruntled mood was the result of still being upset with my ten-year-old son, Michael, from the day before. *When is he going to learn to obey me?* I fumed. *And why does he make the same mistakes over and over? Nothing seems to sink in!* Glancing at the clock, I knew I'd better make the rounds to be sure everyone was up.

As I opened the door to Michael's room, his tousled, curly head peeked out from the covers. With his oh-so-familiar grin, Michael said, "I'm sorry, Mom. I didn't mean to do it." Always before, his sweet smile melted my heart. This time I was determined to teach him a lesson he would not forget.

"Michael, you always say you're sorry. This time I am not going to forgive you."

As I shut the door, satisfied that I'd followed my conviction, I caught a glimpse of his crestfallen face.

Walking away, I could not erase the image. "How can you not forgive him?" the Lord whispered in my ear. "Don't you remember what I have said about forgiving? Rebuke your brother if he sins and forgive him if he is sorry. Even if he wrongs you seven times a day and each time turns again and asks forgiveness, forgive him" (Luke 17:3). God's still, small voice continued, "When you honor my word and obey me, you set the example for Michael."

"Lord," I argued, "forgiving is not easy, especially when someone keeps on offending."

I stood there struggling with mixed emotions, then admitted, "I don't like the way this anger is making me feel. Please! Take it away."

As I felt the feelings of hostility toward Michael slip away, I turned around and headed back to his room. I knew I had to tell him that I forgave him and restore that familiar smile. I also knew I had to ask Michael to forgive me.

Prayer

Father, help me to remember how many times you forgive me every day, how many times I must offend you. Thank you that you are always eager to forgive. Help me to follow your example.

Discovery

Do you find it difficult to continuously forgive someone for his or her mistakes? Do you need to ask them for their forgiveness?

THE CHARGE OF THE
LIGHT BRIGADE

Rescue me, Oh God! Lord, hurry to my aid!
Psalm 70:1

Boxes were everywhere! As I went from room to room, I began to feel overwhelmed with the task before me. *There is so much to do! I don't even know where to begin to unpack.* We had just arrived a few days before from Florida to Michigan with our truckload of four dogs, our carload of kids, and the moving van not far behind.

I had never been very fond of our family of dogs. They were yard dogs, and I never allowed them in the house. I considered them a nuisance, but I tolerated Thor, Brandy, Buck, and Ralph for the kids' sakes. Thor was the first stray to be adopted, then Brandy. Before I knew it, there was a litter of ten puppies! With much cajoling, we gave in to the pleas of the kids to keep Buck and Ralph.

We had moved into a home snuggled into the midst of a state forest, one of the few homes with year-round residents on our side of the lake. The tranquility of the lake setting was beautiful and the solitude was appealing, especially to me. Gazing out the window at the pristine stillness of the lake below, I realized, *No one will even know I am here.* Shaking off a feeling of apprehension, I decided to call David at the office before tackling the impossible task of unpacking. Remembering that our phone service would not be connected for another couple of days, I wondered if I could use my neighbor's phone.

I closed the heavy oak door behind me and started down the dirt road toward my neighbor's house. As the road wound its way through the woods, those apprehensive feelings returned. *With the kids at school and David at work, I really am all alone. I hope my neighbor is home. Thank goodness they are not that far away.*

As I turned to walk up the path to my neighbor's front door, without warning their huge German shepherd charged into the front yard growling ferociously. Freezing in my tracks, I was afraid to move a muscle for fear this raging animal would attack me. "O God!" I cried. "I'm afraid to move! Help me!"

Just as suddenly as the snarling German Shepherd had appeared, I heard a mighty roar from behind me. Thor, Brandy, Ralph, and Buck came charging into the yard, ready, willing, and able to conquer my foe! The menacing shepherd took one look at the charging brigade, put his tail between his legs, and ran for cover. Never was I so glad to see those dogs as they jubilantly pranced and danced around me, rejoicing in their victory.

"Good dogs!" I exclaimed over and over, patting each one on the head. As they proudly marched me back home to safety, a newfound affection began to replace the tolerance I had felt before.

Thor, Brandy, Ralph, and Buck continued their role as the Light Brigade, our sentinels in the midst of the state forest. As soon as one of us stepped outside the door, they stood at attention with wagging tails, ready to accompany us for a walk in the woods or down the dirt road. Their presence was a constant reminder to me of God's loving protection, that no matter where I was or what situation I was in, I was never alone.

Prayer

Thank you, Father, for the many ways you answer when we call out to you for help. Thank you for your protection in distressing situations.

Discovery

Are you aware of God's loving protection? Call out to him, and he will answer!

PERFECT STRANGERS

So let us come boldly to the throne of God
and stay there to receive his mercy and to
find grace to help us in our times of need.

Hebrews 4:16

Moving from the warmth of the Florida sunshine
and its azure blue skies was difficult, especially
going back to the gray skies and colder climate of
Michigan. The chill of fall was in the air, and I
dreaded the onset of winter. I had long forgotten
storm windows, roads covered with drifts of snow,

and bundling up against the cold winter winds. More than that, my heart longed for the warmth of the friendships left behind that had nurtured my soul and spirit over the past several years.

The job opportunity that was offered to my husband, David, made moving impossible to refuse, and so we found our family settling into the home we were renting. An offer had been made to purchase the home with a three-month rental agreement while waiting for the sale of our home in Florida.

The quaint 1920's home, nestled in the midst of a state forest, had the charm of an English cottage. The cascading waterfall from the patio, alongside the ninety-five stone steps that led to the glistening lake below, added a final touch to the tranquil setting. Our mailbox at the ranger station, a mile down the curved, dirt road, added to the solitude. *This hideaway will be the perfect place for me to hibernate through the winter*, I thought.

The one source of comfort for me since the move was the small church we attended. Almost instantly, everyone made us feel loved and accepted. One woman in particular went out of her way to befriend me. My heart was warmed by Janet inviting me to lunch or a movie and always making sure I was included in church activities. It was as if Janet sensed my need to be drawn away from the loneliness of my self-imposed seclusion.

With the holidays fast approaching, time was also drawing near to honor the purchase agreement we had made on our home. With heavy hearts, we knew it was impossible to meet our commitment as the home in Florida had not sold. In just two weeks, we needed to have twenty-five thousand dollars or face the cold reality of hurriedly finding another place to live. On a daily basis we had been asking God to meet our need in the sale of our Florida home. Now David and I agreed the only thing we knew to do was to put this need on the church prayer chain, believing that if anything could move the hands of God, it would be this caring family of God.

A few days later as I sipped my morning coffee and brought my concern once again to God, the phone rang. It was Janet. "George and I have been talking. We've decided we want to take twenty-five thousand dollars out of our retirement fund to loan you the money you will need to buy your home."

I could not contain my amazement at their offer of God's solution to our need. In three months' time, we had gone from being perfect strangers to becoming a part of God's loving family. Suddenly, the harsh winter winds lost their bluster. Snow-covered evergreens were as beautiful as swaying palm trees. The warmth of the Florida sun was replaced with the warmth of God's love.

Prayer

Thank you, Father, for knowing our needs even before we express them. Thank you for putting people in our lives who are willing to be "God with skin on."

Discovery

Do you know someone that needs an answer to their prayers? Are you 'God with skin on'?

FOREVER FRIENDS

I tell you this, if two of you agree down here on earth concerning anything you ask for, my Father in heaven will do it for you. For where two or three are gathered together, I will be right there among them.

Matthew 18:19–20

It was a gray, fall day. *Typical Michigan weather*, I thought, still feeling the effects of missing the Florida sunshine that promised to appear every day. As I finished breakfast, the phone rang.

"I have two tickets to the preview showing of the latest Billy Graham movie," Janet said, "and I want you to come with me." Sensing my hesitation, she continued to urge me to join her. I was still struggling with my desire for seclusion, downcast over leaving Florida. But, because Billy Graham had been so instrumental in my life, I decided to go.

As we came out of the theatre when the movie was over, I waited for Janet to browse the book table in the lobby. Then I saw her, someone I had not seen in a long time. As Sharon approached me with open arms, I began to cry. "You don't want to be here, do you?" she said. I shook my head no. Sharon looked at me with loving eyes and hugged me again. As if time had not passed between us, she said, "When can we get together? I'll call Judy. She'll be so glad to see you too. It will be like old times."

It had been eight years since Sharon, Judy, and I had seen each other. My move to Florida had put the distance between us. We had stayed in touch with Christmas cards, but when I had reluctantly moved back to Michigan, I purposely had not wanted to contact anyone, not even the prayer partners God had provided when my journey with him first began.

My first meeting with Sharon was during a distressing time in my life, much like this one. "There is someone I want you to meet," the pastor had said when I had gone to him for counseling for my marriage, "someone who has had a similar experience. She'll be waiting for you at church next Sunday."

Sharon had reached out to me with open arms and said, "When can we get together?" Sharon then shared that her friend Judy wanted to join us as she had also just begun her journey with God. We had met regularly to encourage and pray for each other that first year before my move to Florida. Now, like before, Sharon was greeting me again with open arms.

Even though I now lived forty miles away instead of in the same town, Sharon and Judy could not wait to come to the house in the woods. After lunch, we began to share our prayer concerns just like before. Being with them again felt wonderful as their positive spirits nurtured mine. I was ashamed that I had put off getting in touch with them. I realized how foolish I was to want to hide myself away from everyone and be absorbed in self-pity. With loving concern, my friends encouraged me to meet the next month, and it soon became a monthly ritual again.

I don't believe in chance meetings. I thank God that he knew my need to reconnect with Sharon and Judy, prayer partners who continued to love and pray for me for three more years and beyond.

Prayer

Thank you, Jesus, for promising to pull up a chair to sit down and join us when two or three of us get together to pray. Thank you for knowing and meeting my need for prayer partners.

Discovery

Do you have someone to pray with on a regular basis? If not, can you think of someone who may need a prayer partner?

Good News

As far as God is concerned, there is a sweet,
wholesome fragrance in our lives. It is the
fragrance of Christ within us, an aroma to
both the saved and the unsaved all around us.

2 Corinthians 2:15

It had been fun getting together with other couples in Miami the weekend before David's company convention began on Monday. Now with
meetings occupying David's time during the day,
I questioned what I could do to entertain myself

besides sitting at the pool. *Lord, there must be a better purpose for me to be here than that.*

No sooner had that thought come to mind when the phone rang. It was Claudia, the wife of one of David's teammates. "Karen, I wonder if you'd do me a favor. I promised a friend who lives on the opposite coast from Miami that I'd drive halfway to meet her for lunch. I don't want to go by myself. Would you be willing to come with me?"

Wow, Lord. That was quick! I'd wanted to get better acquainted with Claudia, so of course I said yes.

As we began to visit in the car for the two-hour drive, Claudia commented, "You know, I've been watching you and David. You seem to have something very special together. I'm curious to know what it is."

I looked over at Claudia, trying to digest what she had said. Watching me? I'd never considered someone might be observing my behavior and my interaction with my husband. I took a deep breath and responded, "David and I have a very special relationship because of Jesus. But it hasn't always been this way." For the next couple of hours I shared how God had restored our marriage.

As we pulled into the parking lot of the restaurant, Claudia said, "I'm starving and I can't wait to see my friend and have lunch, but I wish we could just keep driving because I don't want you to stop talking. I'm so glad we have another couple of hours on the way back so I can continue to hear your story."

After our farewell, Claudia was anxious to pick up where we'd left off, and I began to realize she was now hungry for spiritual things. I silently prayed she would be open to inviting God into her life.

As we pulled into the hotel parking lot, Claudia turned to me and said I'd given her so much to ponder and she was looking forward to spending more time together. I asked if she would like to read through a booklet I had in my purse called *The Four Spiritual Laws*. She took the booklet but shook her head. "No, not now but let me keep it, and I'll look at it later."

During the week, Claudia and I never seemed to have time together alone. A few days later the convention was over. As we flew home, I wondered if I'd have another opportunity to visit with her now that we were both back to our daily routines. A week later Claudia called with an invitation to dinner, giving us time to be alone together again. I looked forward to hearing what she might have to tell me. Would it be good news?

As we enjoyed the evening together, Claudia told me she couldn't stop thinking about what I had shared. Finally one night when she couldn't fall asleep, she dug that little booklet out of her purse. As she read, she became convinced God had an answer for her life and asked Jesus into her heart. That was the best news ever!

Prayer

Thank you, Father, when you are in control of my life, others can see it and be drawn to you.

Discovery

Did you know others are observing you? Are they attracted to the sweet, wholesome fragrance of Christ in you?

Angel Aware

He orders his angels to protect you wherever you go.

Psalm 91:11

The late afternoon sun glistened on the blanket of white covering the frozen lake below my window. Snow had continued to fall since morning, and I was concerned. *Would we make it to church tonight? Maybe we should stay home.* The love and warmth that radiated from our church family was a tremendous comfort that drew us to that fellowship. Neither David nor I wanted to miss being with them to worship God.

Although the narrow dirt roads that wound their way through the forest sheltering our lake home were becoming almost impassable, ever-confident David was ready to go. "Come on, Karen, we can make it," David said as he piled our family into the warmed-up car.

Inching our way down the drive onto the snow-packed road, we slowly began to make our way toward the highway that would take us into town. I was awed by the beauty of the canopy of white and stillness in the midst of the forest. It was as if we were the only ones there.

"Under this snow is a sheet of ice," David commented with concern as he struggled to maneuver the car around another curve.

Suddenly the tranquil mood of the forest was shattered as the car missed the curve, slamming into a looming, massive tree. As I felt the impact propel me forward, I heard David gasp. Tenderly he reached over to pull me back, fearful of what he would see.

Gazing in disbelief at my face, he said, "Thank God, Karen, you're not hurt! But look at the car!"

Slowly I opened my eyes to take in the destruction. As I had flown forward, the top of my head had shattered the windshield, and my forehead and the bridge of my nose had crumbled the dashboard. Hardly believing what I saw, I pulled down the visor mirror to examine my face. Only a tiny cut on the side of my cheek was visible. Something, or someone, had taken the impact and cushioned the blow.

I had read verses in the Bible that claimed God has his angels watching over us, but I never imagined he would have one on duty for me! Several days later, there was still no aftermath from the accident...no broken bones, no headache, no black eyes. There was only the wonder of it all and the assurance of God's constant care.

Prayer

How grateful I am, Father, that you care so much about me that you provide protection from harm, physically and spiritually.

Discovery

Are you aware of God's loving care? Have you felt his angels surrounding you? He orders his angels to protect you wherever you go.

THE ULTIMATE LANDLORD

Don't worry about anything; instead, pray about everything; tell God your needs and don't forget to thank him for his answers. If you do this, you will experience God's peace which is far more wonderful than the human mind can understand. His peace will keep your thoughts and hearts quiet and at rest as you trust in Christ Jesus.

Philippians 4:4–7

Another beautiful day in paradise, I thought as I sipped my morning cup of coffee by the pool. It felt so good to be back. I had missed living in the warmth of the Florida sun and was anxious to sink my toes into the sugar-white sands of the beach and never leave again. As I took the last sip of my coffee, the doorbell rang. David stood at the front door, cradling a large box in his arms. *Where was his company car?*

"Just let me in, Karen. It's okay." *What was he talking about? What's okay?* As he put the box on the floor, overflowing with everything from his office, I heard him say, "I've been fired, and they let four others on my staff go too."

I was stunned! We had just moved from Michigan to Sarasota, Florida, three months before when David had been recruited to be vice president of franchising. Now he and his sales staff had been terminated. I could not believe what I was hearing, yet there seemed to be a calmness about him as he continued to tell me everything would be all right. I could tell he was actually relieved to be out of a very tense environment and his positive nature was assuring him he would find work without a problem.

Four months went by without a promise of a new job. No matter how many résumés David mailed out, no one seemed to need a vice president. The reserve in our savings account was quickly dwindling. "Don't worry; we'll manage," David kept saying. When the pastor of our church came to extend a helping hand, David continued to say, "We'll manage. There are things we can sell to meet our obligations."

Sensing the pride in David's voice, the pastor gently responded, "When you get to Aunt Tillie's antiques, stop. God does not intend for you to sell everything you have. Our Benevolence Fund is there to help you." I knew it was hard for David to accept help from anyone. He had always been the one to give it. Now he had to learn what it meant to receive it.

When our son Michael emptied his bank account to cover a month's rent, we realized we could no longer postpone telling our landlords in Chicago that we could not continue to pay them. We had leased their home for one year until they retired the following summer. *Where will we go? What will we do?* I thought as David dialed their number.

"Don't even think about moving out. We know David will get another job, and when he does, you can pay us then." Were we hearing right? This couple hardly knew us, meeting us for the first time when we signed the lease. As they continued to reassure us, we began to feel God's reassurance. He had obviously handpicked this place of refuge for us months before.

Long walks on the beach continued to help us keep God's perspective. The waves softly lapping at our feet seemed to whisper, "Don't worry, don't worry." The display of his brilliant sunsets sinking into the tranquil waters of the gulf constantly reminded us of his glory and power. Just as he controlled the ebb and flow of the tides, we knew everything in our lives was under his control.

More months went by with still no promise of a job for David. My job at the real estate office helped to put food on the table and gas in the car but could not begin to meet our major obligations. My heart ached for him. I knew he so badly wanted to be the good provider he had always been, and I became so acutely aware of how delicate the male ego can be. I prayed, *Dear God, help me to be sensitive to David's feelings and his emotional needs.* I knew David was drawing his strength from God, and I wanted to be a positive influence for him as well. Our devotion to each other was deeper than ever before.

One morning we woke to the sounds of a storm hurling the waves against the nearby beach. When it was over, we decided to take a walk to view the damage. As we strolled the beach hand in hand, we noticed another couple coming toward us. David squeezed my hand and said, "They look like our landlords from Chicago!" As they caught up to us, we exclaimed, "What a surprise to see you! Are you on vacation?"

We could tell they seemed somewhat embarrassed to see us. "No," they said slowly. "We are renting a condo for a couple of months right over here on the beach. Then, for the summer we are going to housesit for friends." When we began to protest, they continued to say, "We changed our moving plans and didn't want you to think you had to move before the lease is up in August. That's why we didn't tell you we were here." As we said our good-byes and walked away, we were, once again, overwhelmed by their generosity. How could such kindness be extended to us from people we hardly knew?

Prayer

Thank you, Father, for the kindness that comes from people we hardly know. Help us to be willing to extend ourselves to that someone we have just met.

Discovery

Have you felt God's nudge to be kind to someone today?

THE REST OF THE STORY

Take your delight in the Lord and he will
give you the desires of your heart.

Psalm 37:4

David had now been out of work for ten months.
August was fast approaching, and our lease would
soon be terminating. We asked ourselves, *How
will we possibly find another place to live without
income? How will we honor our current landlord's
generosity?* We had been praying for months for
God to give David an opportunity, yet nothing

had happened. Now we were facing the reality of once again not having a place to live.

One morning as I prayed, it occurred to me that I could check on rentals through the real estate office where I worked. Out of curiosity, I began to look at two-bedroom condos, knowing we could manage with a smaller living space. A listing for a condo facing the Gulf of Mexico caught my eye. Could we really have a view of the gulf? I was so drawn to the beauty and tranquility of those sparkling turquoise waters. They seemed to be a visual manifestation of God's promise of peace. A verse from the book of Psalms, "Take your delight in the Lord and he will give you the desires of your heart" (Psalm 37:4), gave me courage. It wouldn't hurt to try.

Not knowing how we could put this together, we went to see the condo. Shades of royal blue, lime green and shocking pink carpeting, outdated wallpaper, and worn printed drapes greeted us as we walked through the door. My perfectionist nature and eye for decorating made me flinch as I took in my surroundings. Yet I realized the floor plan would accommodate our furniture.

And the view of the gulf was beautiful! Could we live here like it was? It really needed to be redecorated. What if! What if the landlord would let us replace the carpeting, drapes and wallpaper in lieu of six months rent and no deposit?

The Realtor had never heard of such a thing. How could she present that kind of an offer to the out-of-town landlord? She became even more frustrated as she tried to interact with him over the phone. He always seemed to want to counteroffer whatever she presented.

Like the sands in an hourglass, our time was running out, now just a few short weeks before we needed to move. Then God's answer came. First, David was offered a job with a franchise company based in Atlanta. Because they needed him to represent them in the field, we could stay in Florida. Then, the frustrated Realtor gave David the opportunity to negotiate with the Chicago landlord. It succeeded in giving us a three-year lease with no increase, no deposit, and six months' free rent in exchange for decorating the condo just the way we wanted it. The old multicolored carpets were gone, replaced with pale cream carpeting and matching drapes. Together with a new kitchen floor and wallpaper, a neutral background was created that would enhance our furnishings and make it feel like home.

As we settled in to enjoy the magnificent view of the gulf, our hearts overflowed with thanksgiving and gratitude. Not only did God meet our needs, he gave us our heart's desire. He was our provider, the ultimate Landlord!

Prayer

Thank you, Father, for being the great Provider, the one we can depend upon to provide all of our needs.

Discovery

Have you thanked God for his provision for you? Do you have an attitude of gratitude?

DAVID VERSUS GOLIATH: A SEQUEL

God turned into good what you meant for
evil.

Genesis 50:20

The phone was ringing. Again. This time it was
2 a.m. The harassing calls were becoming more
frequent, waking us up at all hours of the night.
David reached over to answer the phone. Once
again, no one was on the line. As he settled back

into the warmth of the covers, David said, "It's him again."

Why does this man hate us so much? I thought as I struggled to go back to sleep. He had become a Goliath, doing everything he could get away with to make our lives miserable. If he couldn't physically kill us, he was determined to wound us with words, insults behind the battle lines, hoping to ruin our reputation.

This former business partner was mailing derogatory letters to all of the shareholders of our privately held company, making calls to vendors telling them not to do business with us and sending articles to the local newspaper. Rumors were flying. The final blow was a three-million-dollar lawsuit charging us with fraud.

As David's wife, I loved working alongside him, helping him to build his dream. Here was a man with a vision, not just wanting to find success for himself, but also wanting to build an army of successful business partners. This man's efforts were an attempt to ruin us as he tried to initiate a takeover. Since he had made a major investment in our company, he felt he deserved to run it. He was waging war. David's dream had now become a nightmare.

The dream had begun just a few short years before with a vision to build a new fast-food franchise company. With all of his past experience and the right group of investors, David believed his dream could become a reality. Ethics and integrity were high on the list of his priorities. As he shared his dream, his enthusiasm was contagious, and he soon found himself with the support he needed. With that in mind, David resigned from the Atlanta-based company to embark on his dream.

With the first store opening, excitement mounted! Franchise inquiries started rolling in. But after the elation of success came the deflation of threatening demise. We tried hard to keep the battle between David and his ex-partner under cover. What would people think of us? How would we face those we loved? Even though we were being falsely accused, we knew not everyone would know that or believe it. Then, when the newspaper hit the stands, we were devastated. I wanted to run and hide.

But we had underestimated God. That's exactly what he used to surround us with the loving support he knew we needed. Now many prayers were rising up to heaven on our behalf as friends and family rallied to our side. That Sunday, our pastor took us aside. "What someone meant for evil, God meant for good," he said.

We struggled to survive the financial crisis this conflict caused. When we learned of the enormous cost of a defense attorney, we knew it was impossible to even think of hiring one. "I'm going to have to be our attorney," David said.

David began to gather his weapons. He prayed and prepared by going to the local library, researching file after file, typing page after page to present his counter suit of ten million dollars. I admired his courage to take on this horrendous battle by himself. Yet I knew he wasn't really alone. Goliath had met his match with the David of the Bible; I knew God was with my David as well as he began to gather his own slingshot and pebbles of defense.

Our opponent's attorney scoffed at the audacity of our countersuit, but much to his amazement, the judge accepted it! Now the shoe was on the other foot! It was our turn to tell the world our side of the story.

David could feel the adrenalin rush! How good it felt to at last be the one in control. David was more than ready to fight. He was eager, anticipating it with relish, anxious for revenge!

With this surprising turn of events, our opponent decided to drop his charges against us. He was not prepared to face David. He definitely did not want David to have his day in court. Unlike Goliath, our foe hid himself behind the shield of his attorney.

We could hardly wait for the day we could walk into our opponent's attorney's office to accept the final paperwork dismissing the lawsuit. How we looked forward to gloating over their attempts to ruin us. Despite the odds against us, we had won! It felt so good to be vindicated! We could once again hold our heads up high.

As we walked toward the office, David turned to me and said, "We are going to walk in there with God's love on our faces, not our victory. God is telling me to drop our suit against them.

Even though we have lost control of the company and we don't know what lies ahead, we can put it behind us and walk forward knowing God will be by our side."

I could hardly contain my feelings of elation over our victory, but I knew David was right. God wanted us to show his love and forgiveness, not hatred. So we did.

As we were able to let go of the anger, I began to realize God's vision for the company had been different from ours. His vision was to build a man of character, a new David, another man after God's own heart. In God's eyes, it had been a success.

Prayer

Thank you, Father, that you can help us to love our enemies, those who treat us unfairly and want to hurt us. Thank you that when we do, we become more like you.

Discovery

Is there someone in your life who is being hurtful and mean to you? What do you think would happen if you responded to them with God's love?

TRANQUILITY
AMID TURMOIL

When you draw close to God, God will draw close to you.

James 4:8

I stepped out to the balcony of our condo, drawn by the beauty of the Gulf of Mexico below. The warmth of the sun caressed my body, and I watched its rays skip across the turquoise waters like sparkling jewels. Despite the beauty and tranquility around me, I felt the ugly turmoil of my life whirling inside me, and my heart cried out, *Lord, I don't know how much more I can take! Like the pull of the undertow of the tides below, I feel I'm being pulled under by despair, and I'm drowning!*

As I turned and leaned against the railing, I glanced over at the fichus tree standing in the corner of the balcony. *How amazing for it to have survived the beating of the winter storms, battered and stripped of all its leaves.* I remembered wanting to discard it, knowing it must be dead. Only David's insistence that he would nourish it had kept the tree in place. Now the tree stood tall, proudly displaying its lush grandeur, not only surviving, but growing stronger and more beautiful than before.

Taking in the transformation before me, I realized this was a reflection of my life! *If I trust that you will care for me, Lord, through the storms and beatings of this devastating trial, like this fichus tree, you will bring me through. I won't only just survive, but my character will grow stronger and more beautiful because of it.*

God's words of encouragement from the morning's devotional in Psalms came to mind, speaking to my heart.

> Whoever delights in doing what God wants them to, day and night meditating on his laws and thinking about ways to follow him more closely, are like trees along a river bank bearing luscious fruit each season without fail. Their leaves shall never wither, and all they do shall prosper.
>
> Psalm 1:2–3, paraphrase

I sensed God's peace beginning to fill me, replacing my inner turmoil with his tranquility. God reminded me once again that if I continued to draw close to him, he would draw close to me.

Prayer

Thank you, Father, for giving me your tranquility amid the turmoil and storms of life. Thank you for the peace that passes all understanding.

Discovery

What is beating you down in discouragement? Draw close to God. He promises to draw close to you.

Billy's Pecan Pie

Cheerfully share your home with those who
need a meal.

1 Peter 4:9

What would we have done without Billy's pecan
pie? Not that it was needed as a staple for our
diet, it was everything else that it represented.

"Come on over for dinner," my new friend
Eleanor invited. "I want you to meet my husband,
Bill. You'll love his Southern cooking, especially a

slice of his warm pecan pie topped with a mountain of ice cream!"

Bill and Eleanor could have offered us cheese and crackers, and we would have been delighted to accept their invitation. With David's unemployment, we needed all the encouragement we could get. Our new friends from church seemed to sense that. Along with that generous slice of pecan pie à la mode came many evenings of generous amounts of love and concern carrying us through times of triumph and trials over the next five years.

When David finally found employment with the Atlanta-based company, they were glad. When David decided to leave the company and venture out on a dream of his own, they cheered him on. When David's dream fell apart, they were there to comfort us, each time offering us another generous slice of Billy's pecan pie and their love.

Bill and Eleanor were gracious givers, each in their own way. Eleanor was a charming, genteel lady who loved setting the table with her fine china and sterling silver, making Billy's home cookin' taste even better! On several occasions, they would treat us to dinner at one of their favorite Sarasota restaurants or the yacht club. As a retired dentist, Bill seemed to know everyone in town. He enjoyed greeting the local politicians and giving a gentle chiding to his favorite wait staff. To finish off the evening, Bill loved to spin a tale about the local folk or of his World War II escapades.

Through their friendship, we were repeatedly reminded of the verse from 1 Corinthians 13:7. "If you love someone, you will be loyal to him no matter what the cost. You will always believe in him, always expect the best of him and always stand your ground in defending him." It did not matter what the circumstance, Bill and Eleanor believed in us. The differences in our ages and social status did not seem to matter either. They stood by us with open arms of love and slice after slice of that scrumptious pecan pie à la mode!

When it was time for us to leave Florida, it was difficult for many reasons. Bill and Eleanor's friendship and Billy's pecan pie were at the top of the list.

Prayer

Thank you, Father, for friends that nourish us with their love and concern, helping us to handle the bitter and embrace the sweet.

Discovery

Have you become aware of someone who needs a friend? It could start with an invitation to dinner.

THE BIG TEN

Honor the Lord by giving him the first
part of all your income, and he will fill your
barns with wheat and overflow your wine
vats with the finest wines.

Proverbs 3:9–10

Omaha, Nebraska, was now our home, a far cry
from sunny Sarasota, Florida. Yet we knew God
had provided this opportunity for us to begin
again. David had been hired to direct the franchise sales of a fast-food sandwich company. I

found employment as the assistant to the president as well as to the CEO of a local bank. We settled into a two-bedroom town home and found a new church home that made us feel welcome.

At first, things went well for David as he accomplished the goals set by the owner of the company. He had been hired on salary with a bonus. But, each time the goals were met, the owner would decide to change David's income structure, cutting back on the salary and making David more dependent on commissions. Toward the third year, David was totally on commission.

I, on the other hand, loved working at the bank. On my list of favorite things to do, it got a big ten! Mr. Folda and Mr. Given (my employers) were amiable and easy to work with, often giving me assignments that were out of the ordinary. What fun it was to leave the office early to scour antique shops to furnish the downtown branch, plan parties and open houses, take two-hour lunches to coordinate the company newsletter, and be the bank's ambassador for the Chamber of Commerce.

Toward the end of the year, it was time for my annual review. I was hoping for a generous raise since David's income was so sporadic. I knew my bosses were pleased with how I handled my responsibilities, but I really had no idea of what to expect. During this time of waiting for my review, God began to speak to me on the subject of tithing. Always before, we had given back to God from what we had left over, but God was now impressing upon me that we needed to honor him first. *What about me?* He seemed to be saying. *Don't I deserve a ten?* I knew that since I was the one with dependable income, it would have to begin with me to put God at the top of our list. David was agreeable, and so I began to tithe 10 percent.

The day arrived for my review. Sensing my nervousness, Mr. Given smiled as he invited me into his office. "Karen," he said, "we want you to know we are very pleased with your performance. You have done an excellent job. Mr. Folda and I have given you all tens on your appraisal!" On a more serious note, Mr. Given continued. "We are disappointed that this year we can only offer our employees a five percent raise. We wish it could be more. Then with a big grin crossing his face he said, "However, Mr. Folda and I have talked this over. We have agreed we can each give you five percent, making your actual increase a big ten!"

As I walked back to my desk, I was amazed! It was not just the magnanimous reward I had been given by my employers, it was the realization that in less than a month God had returned the ten percent I had promised to give to him!

Prayer

Father, thank you for your generosity and your faithfulness! Thank you for honoring your promise to reward me when I'm obedient to you.

Discovery

Do you struggle with giving to God before everything else? Test his promise and see what happens!

No Money Down!

All the world is mine and everything in it... I want you to trust me in your times of trouble so I can rescue you and you can give me glory.

Psalm 50:12, 15

It didn't take much coaxing from a headhunter to convince David to make the move from Omaha, Nebraska, to Milwaukee, Wisconsin. He would become the vice president of franchising for another fast-food sandwich company that hoped to build a strong franchise system. David was ready for a change and a new challenge.

As David went for his final interview, I made my list of priorities of what I hoped God would provide in our new home. *Let's see. I would like three bedrooms so we can have a guest room and an office. Next, I would like to have a fireplace, and I'll definitely need an attached garage if I am still going to live in a cold climate! And I don't want to have to pay more than what we are paying for this two-bedroom town home. In fact, Lord, I'd appreciate it if we could find something for one hundred dollars less a month.* Looking over my list, I suddenly wondered, *Am I asking too much? It sounds like I'm giving God a Santa's wish list!*

"You won't believe this, Karen," David exclaimed on his return home that weekend. "The co-owner of the company in Milwaukee offered to rent us his four-bedroom home with a fireplace, an attached garage, a six-car detached garage, plus a pool! And, you won't believe the price!" The price was exactly what I had prayed for, and the house, it was so much more!

"What an awesome God we have," I exclaimed, as I shared with David what I had asked for. Happily settling into our new home and community, we thanked God for his abundant, indulgent provision.

Toward the end of the year, the owner asked if we would like to buy the house. His accountant was telling him he needed to sell and we could have it for fifty thousand dollars down. *He must be kidding!* I thought. *He might as well have asked us for a million*! Struggling to overcome the financial difficulties we had suffered in Florida, we had no extra money to even consider buying a home. We were devastated to think we would have to move. As we contemplated what to do, the owner offered a suggestion. "Why not ask a bank to loan you fifty thousand dollars? The house is worth three to four times that amount, and I'll take a second mortgage for the balance." The bank agreed it was a good deal for them, and we thought it was a great deal for us! Now all we had to worry about were the closing costs.

"I hope they won't be more than we can handle," David commented as we drove to the bank.

God must have had a smile on his face as he thought, *Not to worry! I have this all taken care of too. Don't you remember the world is mine and all that is in it? Just watch!*

Since the owner needed to put six months of escrow money into our account for taxes on the house, the bank simply deducted all of the closing costs from the escrow account! Buying the house did not cost us a cent. No money down!

Prayer

Father, you are indeed an awesome God! Thank you that your answers to our needs are above and beyond our comprehension.

Discovery

Have you called upon God in your day of trouble? He promises to deliver!

LET THE GOOD TIMES ROLL!

Kind words [and parties] are like honey, enjoyable and healthful.

Proverbs 16:24

There she was, sitting right in front of me in church. Betty Ann turned to me with a friendly smile. As we became acquainted, I learned she lived alone. Arthritis was making it more difficult for her to walk to the store and bank, climb the stairs to her apartment, and keep up with laundry and house-keeping. When I offered to come and help, she threw her arms around me, exclaiming, "You are an answer to my prayers!" Little did I know how much of a blessing she would become to me.

Betty Ann loved having company and sharing memories of her childhood and married life. She was childless and had been a widow for forty years. Very quickly I became an adopted daughter.

One day as I entered her apartment, Betty Ann was sitting in the middle of the living room, sorting through all of her things. Knowing I collected blue and white patterned dishes, she held up four cereal bowls. "Here, I want you to have these. Every morning I made my husband's oatmeal, serving it to him in these bowls. I want you to have them to remember me."

I sensed Betty Ann was in the process of making peace with her life and with her death. As we talked, she shared that she had just visited with the pastor about her funeral arrangements. When he asked if she wanted to have refreshments served afterward, she said, "You mean there will be a party and I won't be able to enjoy it?"

As Betty Ann continued to talk, I realized no one had ever given her a party, not even a birthday party. "Let's plan a party, Betty Ann!" I said. "We can have it around your birthday, but you and I will know it's really your going-away party."

"Could we really do that?" she asked with excitement mounting in her voice. "There are so many people I haven't seen for so long!"

Invitations were mailed, the church hall was decorated, and people came from miles away. As each one came to pay their respects, Betty Ann's delight permeated the room like the fragrance of a sweet perfume. The following week Betty Ann was still bubbling over, talking about the party from the moment I came till the time I left. As we visited, I asked, "Betty Ann, have you given any more thought to moving to the retirement community we had talked about?"

"Let's go see what it looks like," she said. Walking into the lobby, Betty Ann exclaimed, "This is so beautiful! I can't believe I didn't want to come before. Let's go sign the lease papers and my new lease on life!"

Sensing her delight, I was delighted that we would be friends a while longer.

Prayer

Thank you Father, for giving us opportunities to be involved in other people's lives. Thank you that the blessings given come back to us a hundred fold.

Discovery

Who do you know that needs your tender loving care?

In Style with God

Let him have all your worries and cares for he is always thinking about you and watching everything that concerns you.

1 Peter 5:7

It was a beautiful spring day, unusually warm for April in Wisconsin. I opened the patio door of the hotel room and stepped outside. *The sun feels so good*, I thought, wishing I could linger a while longer. *I had better get dressed. It's almost time for the convention to begin and David will need my help.*

His company conventions were always enjoyable, and I looked forward to the evening's program. Even though this one was being held in a conference center close to home, we had decided to stay at the hotel to be closer to all the activities David had planned. *I won't need my purse tonight. I'll just take my key*, I thought as I finished dressing and hurried to join David.

The evening was festive and fun, putting us in lighthearted spirits as we returned to our room for the night. As we entered the room, I looked for my purse to put away the key. "David, do you see my purse anywhere?" I asked. "I thought I had left it on the credenza, but it's not there!" Glancing around the room, I realized what I had done. How could I be so careless to leave the patio door unlocked, drapes open and the lights on, revealing my purse in full view? Now it was midnight and pouring rain. Whoever stole my purse would not care that it was my favorite designer handbag. As soon as they took what they wanted, they would toss it aside.

"We had better call the police and credit-card companies right away," David said as he tried to console me. "You can get a new driver's license in the morning while I attend the convention sessions."

With less enthusiasm than the day before, I joined David for the evening festivities, still blaming myself for being so careless. *How could I put myself in jeopardy of someone misusing my credit cards? What a nuisance it was to have to replace them!*

When the convention ended the next day, I left for a luncheon I was scheduled to attend and David went back to the office. Driving to the restaurant, I still struggled with the loss of that designer handbag. As I prayed, I realized I needed to give it up as lost. After all, in the bigger scheme of life, what did it really matter? This was just a personal thing that was important to me, nothing of real significance.

As the luncheon program was about to begin, I was asked to take a phone call from David. Someone had found my purse! Dialing the number, I realized I knew the person I was calling! When my friend answered, she told me her husband was in their backyard the day before and noticed something by the side of the road that ran behind their property. It was my designer handbag, in perfect condition. It was as though it had just been placed there, not tossed aside in the pouring rain the night it had been stolen. The only thing missing was the money from my wallet!

In that moment, I knew that God cared about everything in my life. Surely if the designer of the universe cared about the loss of a designer hand-bag, he would care about the more monumental things that really mattered.

Prayer

Thank you, Father, that you care even about the smallest details in our lives, that you are always thinking about us and watching over us.

Discovery

Do you hesitate to ask God's help for the small things that concern you? Remember, he loves everything about you.

My Butterfly Friend

A cheerful heart does good like medicine.
Proverbs 17:22

Carol and Fred were newcomers to our church. I wanted Carol to feel welcome and invited her to attend a ladies' luncheon with me. Carol hesitated. "I have a rare heart disease that can only be treated with experimental medication. I never know when I'm feeling up to doing something. I'd really like to but I'm sorry, I'd better not plan on it."

I was disappointed. I had immediately liked her. I wanted to get to know her better. She had such beautiful sparkling blue eyes and a smile that belied the fact there was anything physically wrong.

As the months went by, we would greet each other in church, but each time an invitation was extended to do something, she would refuse. Still, Carol remained on my mind and heart, and I decided to try once more. This time I invited her to attend a Bible study with me at another friend's home. "I don't even know if I could concentrate on the lesson. The heart medication slows everything down." Then softly she said, "I think I'd like to try."

As the weeks went by, Carol began to respond to the love being shared at the study. Even when she wasn't feeling her best, she made the effort to attend. We were delighted to see the beginning of her transformation. God was touching her heart in more ways than one.

One morning as we visited in the church foyer, my friend Darlene joined us. "Let's invite Carol to our pajama party!" Grown women having a pajama party? The idea had come to me as a way of not being lonely while my husband traveled on business. Why not have my friend Darlene come and spend the night? It seemed we never had enough time together. There was always so much to talk, laugh and pray about. "That sounds like fun! I'll do it!" Carol said, much to her surprise and ours.

She came through the door with her arms loaded, going back to the car to get even more. Carol not only brought her pajamas but her own pillow, comforter, teddy bear, and everything else she needed to feel at home away from home. The three of us talked, prayed, and giggled until the wee hours of the morning and after a late breakfast, talked into the afternoon, still in our pajamas.

Many more pajama parties followed. Each time the guest room Carol occupied became more and more like home. Finally, she no longer needed to bring her pillow, comforter and all the other things she clung to for solace. Like a butterfly, she was in the process of emerging from her cocoon.

Miraculously, more adventures began. We started going on little outings, then bigger and bigger ones. The highlight of our escapades was the three of us taking an overnight trip to attend the *Oprah Show*. Once again, I was amazed at how far Carol had come from that first day we had met. Eventually, trips on her own were second nature to her.

But when her daughter called announcing Carol's impending grandmother-hood, some of Carol's old doubts resurfaced: "Can I be the kind of grandmother I want to be? I want to have fun with my babies. I want to babysit them, rock them, hold them, and play with them."

Carol's concerns for being physically able to care for her new grandson soon faded. The joy of holding him filled her heart to overflowing. And with the second and third grandchild, her heart's capacity and her ability tripled!

Last week she called, exclaiming, "I'm going to Europe! Five days in Paris and five days in Austria to celebrate Holly and Andy's anniversary. They want me to come to watch the grandkids while they enjoy evenings out. My doctor has given me permission to go! Can you believe it?"

Yes, I can believe it because it's true! A cheerful heart is really the best medicine, capable of transforming anyone.

Prayer

Thank you, Father, for your transforming power at work within us through the Holy Spirit. Thank you for helping us to depend upon you for our physical and spiritual strength.

Discovery

Have you discovered the joy of the Lord as your strength?

A Friend in Lillehammer

O Lord, you have examined my heart and
know everything about me. You know when
I sit or stand. When far away, you know my
every thought. You chart the path ahead
of me and tell me where to stop and rest.
Every moment you know where I am.

Psalm 139:1–3

We had been invited to attend the Winter
Olympics in Lillehammer, Norway. The invita-

tion had come from one of the vendors of the company David worked for. Thirteen couples would be treated to an all-expense paid trip for ten eventful days. We knew it was the chance of a lifetime. This would be our first trip abroad, and with only a few short weeks to get the necessary passports and heavy winter clothing, the anticipation was exhilarating.

Now here we were, winding through the snow-covered mountains on our way back to the ski lodge. Everyone on the bus was exhausted from the excitement of the day's events. Everyone except me. As I glanced out the window, I was overwhelmed by the vastness of the countryside and from being so far away from home. *Lord, do you even know where I am?*

David had been excited since the day we had received the invitation and was enjoying every minute of the festivities. As was his nature, he felt quite at home with everyone from all over the world. I, on the other hand, had felt intimidated from the beginning at the idea of leaving the comfort of my home and my country. Now that I was here, I felt so alone.

I looked to David for comfort, but he was fast asleep. Glancing hurriedly about the bus, I realized I was the only passenger awake. I tried to focus on the music the bus driver was listening to, although the Norwegian songs were just as foreign to me as the surrounding countryside. Suddenly, the music changed to a tune I recognized!

As I listened to the words of the song, my heart and mind were comforted. I realized that God knew exactly where I was and was watching over me, reminding me that even though I was far away from home, I was never far away from him. I glanced around to see if anyone else heard the music, but everyone was still fast asleep. Even the bus driver didn't seem to notice when the last chords of the song *How Great Thou Art* resounded through the bus in English and the Norwegian folk songs flooded the airwaves once again.

Prayer

Thank you, Father, that no matter where we are, you are there. Thank you for wrapping your arms around us whenever we need a hug.

Discovery

Have you ever felt alone in a crowd? Does your heart long for a hug from a friend? Snuggle up to God, your loving Father.

PERSONALITY WITH
A CAPITAL P!

I can do everything God asks me to with the
help of Christ who gives me the strength
and power.

Philippians 4:13

As I put down the book I had been reading,
something on the back page caught my eye.
"Are you fascinated by the new understanding
the Personalities have given you? Have you been

wanting to teach this life-changing material to others? Now you have the opportunity to become a Certified Trainer of the popular Personality concepts by attending one of our workshops." *Fascinated?* I thought. *I'm spellbound!*

I couldn't seem to get my hands on enough books that had been written by Florence and Marita Littauer. They had opened the door of understanding to me, not only understanding who I was, but understanding why everyone else didn't think exactly like me. As I applied what I was learning, I saw what a tremendous difference it was making in my relationships. It was giving me the ability to be more forgiving, more tolerant of the differences that I saw in my husband, children, and friends. To think that I could be personally trained by the authors of these books was exhilarating. I quickly called the number to request the brochure before I lost my nerve.

As I read over the material, I began to question myself. *What makes you think you can do this? First of all, you have to fly out to California all by yourself, meet a perfect stranger at the airport to ride to the conference center, and then meet lots of other perfect strangers who will be attending the work-shop. At the end of the three days of training, you'll have to stand up in front of everybody and give a presentation. And, not just in front of everybody, but in front of the authors of these books! And you are no spring chicken. In just a few months you'll be cel-ebrating your sixtieth birthday!*

The very thought of it made me shudder. I had learned a lot about myself in the course of reading about the Personalities. For instance, I was a perfectionist with a capital *P!* That meant my presentation would need to be absolutely per-fect so no one could find any fault. I would have to be perfectly attired so they could find no fault with the way I looked.

Maybe I could just audit this. After all, I'm really only interested in doing this for my own benefit. The thought of auditing the workshop soothed my nerves and calmed the swarm of butterflies attacking my stomach.

As I began to fill out the registration form, the other part of my personality began to rear its head, that "take charge and be up to a challenge" part of me. *Wait a minute,* it said. *What if God really wants you to teach this stuff to somebody else? You're going to need some credentials! You might as well go for it and give it all you've got.*

As the landing gear of the aircraft hit the California runway, I found my apprehension giving way to excitement. The drive to the San Bernardino Mountains was beautiful, and the lodge extended a warm welcome. *I could actually enjoy this*, I thought as I unpacked my bags.

That evening Florence and Marita gathered us together for a get-acquainted session.

The room was filled with excited chatter and laughter. Then Florence asked, "Why did you come to this workshop?" The outgoing, bubbly personalities couldn't wait to say how excited they were to become speakers and to even become writers! As I listened I thought, *What am I doing here? I don't want to do any of those things*!

The next three days were packed with even more fascinating information than I had read in the books. The other participants were friendly and as eager for encouragement as I was for the impending presentation.

Five minutes. It only has to be a five-minute presentation. You can do it; you can survive it, I kept telling myself. My perfect outfit was neatly pressed, hanging in the closet, awaiting the big moment. I had read and re-read my notes. There wasn't anything more I could do but pray I would remember what to say. As I dressed, I glanced over at the bedside table. I reached down and picked up the card of encouragement my friend Carol had given me before I left. Her vote of confidence, along with God's, pushed me out the door.

It's over, I thought, as I breathed a sigh of relief. *I have survived!* All the butterflies had lined up in perfect formation, and when I opened my mouth to speak, the words had tumbled out in the right order. Then I realized I had done more than survived. I had conquered my fears.

Prayer

Thank you, Father, for giving us new opportunities to become more than what we are today. Thank you that you never ask us to step out without stepping right along with us.

Discovery

Are you being pushed out of your comfort zone to attempt something new for God? Remember, you can do anything with Christ, who will give you the strength and power.

HOME SWEET HOME

Search me Oh God and know my heart, what is way inside, the real me. Try me, test me and know my way, how I behave and get along with others. If there be any offensive way in my actions and moods that offend or hurt other people, please help me to change.
paraphrase of Psalm 139:23–24

David and I had been empty-nesters for a long time. Now we were thinking of sharing a new home in Texas with our son Michael and his new bride, Erin. Our ten-year-old grandson, Tyler, would be claiming a bedroom on the weekends as he came for visits. And, for the first time, we would have a house dog because Chelsea, an adorable Shiatsu, was also part of the package.

Will this really work? I wondered. What would my reaction be to a dog wanting to take over the furniture and, perhaps, even my lap? Would I be able to tolerate their choice of music, and how would I get along with a daughter-in-law I hardly knew?

I knew it would be extremely important to find a home that could accommodate all of us, a home that would give each of us not just elbow room and privacy but one that would allow for the differences in our personalities. My husband's strong, take-charge personality would want to be in control. I knew my perfectionist nature would want everything perfectly in place. Michael's easygoing nature would still find it difficult to give up some of his independence. Erin's outgoing, fun-loving personality would be anxious to make it work. We were all hoping it would be a win-win situation as we helped each other out financially.

The two-story house with the master suite on the first floor seemed to be the perfect solution. It would give David and me all the living space we wanted and allow Mike, Erin, and Tyler to have the three-bedroom, two-bath, family-room space upstairs. What could be better! And surely we could share the kitchen, as there were cupboards galore. Even the built-in desk had two drawers!

This could have been a potential war zone for two women with totally opposite operational modes, but Erin and I were delighted to share the cooking and cleaning, taking turns different nights of the week. I rounded out the menus by remembering Michael's favorite childhood recipes that put a smile on his face after a hard day's work. We learned to juggle laundry schedules and even share the telephone line. Yet the best thing we learned was how to share ourselves.

"I'm so glad you are here," Erin would often say to me as she came home from teaching. "I just need to talk about what happened at school today. I need your advice." I loved hearing that as I had so wanted to learn the art of mothering without smothering.

Tyler's favorite weekend pastime was to challenge all of us to one of his favorite board games and to present us with a concert as he practiced his saxophone. Chelsea, that loveable dog snuggling up in my lap, would often sing along as she tried to match the resonant sounds with her own.

Now the house is quiet as another change has taken place. With Michael, Erin, Tyler, and Chelsea now settled into a place of their own, David and I are adjusting to a home with too much space. Knowing it was time for them to make the move, we all can take pleasure in also knowing we learned to live together and love each other beyond our expectations.

Prayer

Father, thank you for giving us opportunities to share our lives with others. Thank you that through your love, we can accept others as they are and learn to change ourselves. When differences become irritations, I can ask you to intervene because I know they are not intentional.

Discovery

Have you considered that someone else's difference of opinion doesn't make them wrong, just different? What changes has God been asking you to make?

My Darling Daughter

Let us stop just saying we love ... let us really love ... and show it by our actions.

1 John 3:18

"Will I ever have a positive relationship with my daughter?" I questioned once again.

"Wait until she's twenty-one," a friend advised. "Everything will change then."

Wait until she's twenty-one? That sounded like an eternity! I wanted to enjoy my daughter now, but that seemed impossible as Susan struggled with being a teen. We could not agree on anything, and with Susan striving for her independence, we were fighting over everything. Like the flower, my black-eyed Susan had been a delight to enjoy. Now Susan's dark brown eyes flashed daggers that could pierce the soul. *What has happened to the darling little girl I knew before, Lord? I want her back! I don't even think this girl likes me, and I'm not sure I like her either.*

"Loving and liking are not the same, Karen," I felt God whisper to my heart. "Picture Susan through my eyes, not yours. Then you'll be able to act lovingly toward her no matter how she responds to you. Remember, my love covers a multitude of faults."

Easier said than done, I thought each time I faced a confrontation with Susan. Yet each time I asked God for his love to replace my inadequacy, he gave it. Still, clashes were eminent and frequent, making us realize there needed to be space between us. More than once, Susan found herself living with another family until she wanted to come back home.

A few years passed, and Susan became a senior in high school. Our move back to Michigan from Florida had not been easy for her, but somehow Susan sensed that my despondency over the move was stronger than hers, and I began to feel her empathy. Cracks were showing in my veneer of self-sufficiency, revealing a part of me Susan hadn't previously recognized. In the revelation, a friendship began to emerge, and we both found ourselves looking forward to spending time with each other.

Adjusting to her new surroundings, Susan began to make new friends. One in particular became that someone special with whom she would choose to spend the rest of her life.

One afternoon as plans were being made for the wedding, I became overwhelmed with the thought of her leaving. *This is happening much too fast and too soon for me, Lord. Susan and I have just begun to enjoy each other's company, making up for lost time. I'm not ready to give her up to someone else.*

As Susan continued to talk about her wedding, I attempted to put my thoughts aside and concentrate on what she was saying. Suddenly

I heard, "Mom, I want you to be my matron of honor. You're the best friend I have."

Several years have gone by with many miles between us. With every birthday and Mother's Day, a special card arrives from Susan. With our move to Texas bringing us right around the corner from each other, this Mother's Day is no exception. Once again tears brim as I read her card.

> Mom, no one has to tell me how lucky I am to have you, because I've known for a long time. When I remember everything you've done for me, I realize that you're not only a wonderful mom, you're also a remarkable woman. You've taught me so much about living, loving, and giving, and those are things I'll never forget. Please don't ever think that I don't appreciate and love you, because I do...with all my heart. Happy Mother's Day. I love you, Sue.

Prayer

Thank you, Father, for your love that overcomes the obstacles and barriers that prevent us from having a positive relationship. Help us to show your love by our actions.

Discovery

Are you in a struggling relationship? Try to picture that person through God's loving eyes.

THE CHRISTMAS ROSE

Always keep on praying.

1 Thessalonians 5:17

It had been several days since he left. The rose on the kitchen window continued to remind me of his visit. The softly curled petals, like scarlet velvet, were almost just as fresh as when the rose was given.

"Which hand do you want, Mamma?" he had said, impishly hiding his gift behind his back.

The note propped against the bud vase brought a smile to my heart as I read, "I love you, Mom. Keith." The whimsical smiley face drawn under his name brought another smile. My thoughts return to the phone call just a few weeks before.

"I'll be home for Christmas, Mom. This time I'm going to make it. This time it isn't going to be if only in my dreams."

It has been five years since Keith had been able to come home for the holidays. Each past year was a dream unfulfilled. Each year his gift was sent to a different address but the same destination, the county jail. Like thorns on a rose, his costly mistakes pricked my heart. This year, it was different. This year, he made it home. And, this year, I sensed a difference in Keith.

"Here I am!" he yelled, waving us over as our car swung into the airport pickup area. Wrapping his arms around me in a bear hug, he squeezed me as tight as he could. It had been so long, and it felt so good. As we embraced, we both sensed this week would go by much too fast.

As Keith began to unpack his duffel bag and settle into the guest room, he turned to me.

"Every day I ask God to help me to be a blessing instead of a curse," he said. "I have been a curse too long. I remember the things I learned as a child, things you taught me and what I learned in Sunday school. Mom, I'm coming back to God."

This wasn't the first time I had heard those words from my prodigal son. I so much wanted to believe them to be true as I had hoped so many times before. Each time, I'd had to let him go. Each time I'd had to let him fall, knowing God would be the only one who could really help him.

This time, though, I sensed something different when Keith spoke those words of coming back to God. There seemed to be a lightheartedness about Keith, as though his spirit had been freed. Could it be that all those years of praying and giving him back to God were finally paying off? So many times I had felt like giving up.

He delighted in the Christmas season, his peals of laughter ringing through the house, lifting my spirit. Gladly he welcomed back the Christmas traditions long remembered as a child. Eager to apply his artistic talents to the annual cookie baking, he taught his nephews the creative art of cutting out original designs. Licking the icing from his fingers was just as much fun as he remembered as he hummed along with the Christmas carols.

There was also a tenderness about Keith that I hadn't seen before, a genuine desire to please others. I often heard him say, "I don't need any presents, just your p-r-e-s-e-n-c-e," as he spelled it out with a grin.

"Let me cook for everyone before I leave," Keith said one evening to the amazement of all. His brother and sister quickly agreed that it would be a treat. Encouraged by the affirmation, Keith and I enjoyed shopping together for the special items needed for his gourmet dinner.

Anxious to talk about God, Keith and I read the Bible and prayed together. In my mind, I had often pictured holding his hand in prayer. I could hardly believe that it was really happening.

One evening as we sat by the warmth of the hearth, Keith talked about his desire to benefit from his mistakes. "I haven't gone through everything for nothing," he said. "There's a reason for it. I want to help kids avoid making the same mistakes I've made." Sharing his dream of providing a place where kids could turn their lives around, Keith envisioned a haven where music and art and God would be a positive influence in their transformation. It felt good to be warmed by his dreams.

Too soon, our week was over. His bags were packed. It was time to catch his flight back to Georgia. Wrapping his arms around me one last time, he whispered, "Pray for me, Mom. I still have some bad habits to kick."

"One step at a time," I replied. "One step at a time."

Could it be that my prodigal son had really come home this time? Once again, I found myself drawn back to the rose on the kitchen window sill. As I took in the beauty of the scarlet petals, I was reminded of the one who could keep him ... Jesus, the Rose of Sharon.

Prayer

Father, thank you for answering my prayers and drawing my child closer to you. Help me to continue to believe your Word that says you will complete the work you have begun in their life. Help me to be faithful in prayer and encouragement.

Discovery

After praying so long for your prodigal child, have you felt like giving up? Continue to trust God. Seek prayer support from others who will lift up you and the needs of your child.

FLIGHT CONNECTION

Jesus said, "I am leaving you with a gift, peace of mind and heart. And the peace I give isn't fragile like the world gives. So don't be troubled or afraid."

John 14:27

"I really can't believe we made this flight," David said as we settled into our seats. "With the blizzard hitting the New York area, I thought for sure they'd cancel."

After spending a week on the island of St. Maarten, we were heading home. We would pick up passengers on the neighboring island of Antigua, then change planes in Newark, New Jersey, before reaching our final destination of Houston, Texas.

"Won't it be nice if no one wants the window seat on this flight," I said, smiling at my husband. "I know you'd like to have more elbow room, and I'm looking forward to reading the rest of the manuscript I promised to review." Antigua was only a twenty-four minute flight from St. Maarten, giving me just enough time to dig out the stories as the plane took off and then landed on the picturesque island.

Engrossed in my reading, I didn't notice the young man standing in the aisle. "Excuse me," he said. "I believe the window seat is mine." As he waited for us to move out of his way, he asked, "Do you mind if I sit there?"

Trying to hide our disappointment in losing that coveted extra space, we quickly exclaimed, "Of course not. Why do you ask?"

"Not everyone is comfortable sitting next to a black man," he said as he made his way to the seat.

Concerned that we may have offended him, I began to engage him in conversation. As we talked, I discovered he was born on the island and earned his living on the yachts that ventured into the beautiful Antigua harbors. One of the vacationing families had extended an invitation to him to spend Christmas in New York.

"Why am I leaving my beautiful paradise island?" he questioned as he began to wipe the nervous perspiration collecting on his face. "I have rebooked this flight so many times! I almost changed my mind again today." Over and over he voiced his concerns of leaving home and his discomfort in flying. As the plane began to make its way down the runway for takeoff, he looked at me and asked, "Are you Christians?"

With a smile I said, "Yes, we are."

Tears began to stream down his face as he looked into mine. "I knew it. I could feel the peace of God coming from you."

I quickly tried to reassure him that God was holding us in the palm of his hand for the flight.

As the engines roared for takeoff, I reached over for David's familiar hand of comfort. Suddenly, I felt my other hand being tightly clasped. Tears were now streaming down my own face as I realized what was taking place. Like a current flowing through us, God's spirit was connecting us with his love, a love that crosses barriers placed by people of different races, cultures, and countries. How beautiful it was to see God bring a feeling of peace and unity in just a matter of minutes. How amazing it was to realize we both had almost missed our flight connection.

He relaxed and settled back in his seat. "My name is Ronnie." We continued to talk. "A lot of people don't believe that God exists," he said.

I began to realize there was a deeper issue on his mind. "Are you questioning your own faith?" I asked. He nodded. "God can reveal himself every day in small ways. I'm reading stories of how he has done that in many people's lives. I've written a story too. Would you like to read it?" Ronnie quickly reached over for the pages in my hand.

As Ronnie read, the expression on his face softened. "I see what you mean. We just need to trust him day to day for our needs and our answers to prayers." Looking over at me, Ronnie smiled and said, "He has already done that for me today. God has given me you."

This time tears were welling up in both of our eyes as we realized God has wanted each of us to keep his flight connection.

Prayer

Thank you, Father, that we can trust you day to day and moment by moment knowing that you hear and answer our prayers. When we do this, we can feel the peace of mind and heart that you promise to give.

Discovery

In what way has God revealed himself to you today? In what way can you be a part of God's answer to someone else's prayer?

THE WAITING ROOM

Yet the Lord still waits for you to come to him so he can show you his love, for the Lord is faithful to his promises. Blessed are all those who wait for him to help them.

Isaiah 30:18

Once again I enter the room. It's familiar to me now. Settling into the easy chair, I wonder, *How many times have I been here before? Far too many to count.* I remind myself, *Lord, each time I've been*

asked to enter your waiting room, I've discovered you
have a purpose.

Glancing around the room, I notice a new
plaque has been hung among the others that I've
read so often before. Drawing closer, I read "The
Lord is waiting to be gracious." *Oh, merciful and
compassionate God,* my heart cries. *Help me to continue to wait for your answers!*

I sigh and sink back into the cushions, now
worn and stained from years of use. *Will I ever
learn the secret of contentment no matter what situation I am in? One moment I find myself singing
hymns I haven't remembered in years. In the next,
I become overwhelmed with anxiety, wondering if
an answer will ever come. Then, as I sit quietly, you
whisper a promise, and I remember. I remember how
you answered my needs time after time, from one
impossible situation to the next, from the smallest,
most insignificant concern to the most monumental,
and I am truly blessed!*

Wiping the tears from my eyes, I notice another
plaque is slightly crooked and dusty. *This one has
been hanging on the wall a long time, Lord, yet I can
see its message is as fresh and relevant as your latest*

one. "I waited patiently for God to help me; then he listened and heard my cry" (Psalm 40:1).

I stand back and take another look, realizing the room is papered with his promises. "Don't be impatient. Wait for the Lord and he will come and save you" (Psalm 27:14).

Another speaks to my heart. "I wait expectantly trusting God to help for he has promised. I long for him more than sentinels long for the dawn" (Psalm 130:5–6).

Then another. "The Lord is wonderfully good to those who wait for him, to those who seek him" (Lamentations 3:25–26).

As I quietly close the door behind me, I ask, *Lord, is the secret of contentment hidden in the process of waiting patiently?*

Prayer

Oh, most merciful and gracious Father, thank you for inviting me into your waiting room to learn firsthand the purpose you have for my life. Thank you for your promises.

Discovery

Do you find it hard to wait on God? Remember, he is waiting to be gracious to you.

WHO ME, LORD?

Everyone enjoys giving good advice, and
how wonderful it is to be able to say the
right thing at the right time.

Proverbs 15:23

It all started with an idea. Not my idea, that's for
sure! "Why don't you put the stories you have
shared with me in writing?" my friend Carol
commented while visiting from Milwaukee.

I looked at her, not quite believing what I'd
heard. *What made her think I could write something*

that someone else would want to read? Telling someone what God had done in my life was one thing, but attempting to write it down was another.

Carol kept on talking as if my reaction of disbelief had not registered. "Now that you're sharing your home with your daughter-in-law, Erin, you have a built-in mentor and editor, your own personal coach! Didn't you tell me Erin is an English and creative writing teacher and has had her own stories published? You really need to take advantage of what God has provided."

Just a few days before, Erin had made a similar comment. "I'll help you, Karen. I know you can do it."

Writing was something I never would have thought of doing. Yet a verse from the Bible came to mind with Erin's initial encouragement. "Be very careful never to forget what you have seen God doing for you. May his miracles have a deep and permanent effect upon your lives. Tell your children and your grandchildren about the glorious miracles he did" (Deuteronomy 4:9).

Well, I do like the idea of sharing the glorious miracles God has done in my life and passing them down to my children and grandchildren. Maybe I could put a collection of stories together in a notebook for them.

Sitting at the computer, one story after another seemed to spill out over the keyboard. True to her word, Erin made suggestions and corrections, helping to bring each story to fruition.

"I think we need to start sending some of these essays out to publishers," Erin commented as we put the final touches on a story.

Who would I send them to? I wondered. I remembered seeing a promotion for the God's Way book series from CLASServices. I wouldn't know until I tried. If anything was going to happen, it would only be because God had opened the door with the encouragement received from Carol and Erin. Several months went by. Then one day as I checked my e-mail messages, there it was! "Your story, 'A Marriage Made in Heaven,' has been accepted for publication in *God's Way for Women*." I could hardly believe it! My story would be one of thirty-eight stories of women living a life of purpose God's way.

Erin and Carol were even more excited than I was. Giving me a hug, Erin said, "I love the art of writing, but you have a purpose larger than yourself. I am blessed to be a part of the contribution."

When I called Carol to share the good news, she said, "I cannot wait to see your own book for sale on the bookshelves!"

Wait a minute! Here she goes again with another crazy idea. Who would want to buy my book? It is one thing to have a story included in a collection with other writers, but why would anyone want to buy a book of my stories? I am not famous. I am just an ordinary woman trusting an extraordinary God.

"Maybe, just maybe," God seemed to say, "an ordinary woman just like you would want to read your book, hoping to discover how she, too, could become a woman of purpose trusting an extraordinary God."

Prayer

Thank you, Father, for friends who nurture us with words of encouragement. Friends, who continue to spur us on to finish the task set before us.

Discovery

Reach out today and touch someone with a word of encouragement. You'll be glad you did and so will they!

The Gift

Do you long for significance and struggle with meaning in your life? Are you wondering how to find it?

God has a gift for you. The Bible confirms that God loves you so much that he sent his only son, Jesus, to earth to be the sacrifice for your sins. If you accept this gift, you will not only open yourself up to the abundant life he promises here and now, but you will enjoy heaven with him forever.

> For God loved the world so much that he gave his only son so that anyone who be-

lieves in him shall not perish but have eternal life.

John 3:16 (TLB)

Yes, all have sinned, all fall short of God's glorious ideal, yet now God declares us "not guilty" of offending him if we trust in Jesus Christ, who in his kindness freely takes away our sins.

Romans 3:23 (TLB)

Jesus said, "My purpose is to give life in all its fullness."

John 10:10 (TLB)

Jesus said, "Look! I've been standing at the door and constantly knocking. If anyone hears me calling him and opens the door, I will come in and fellowship with him and he with me."

Revelations 3:20 (TLB)

Prayer

Dear Lord Jesus,

I acknowledge that up to this point there has been an emptiness in my life. I now realize that only you can fill that empty place and give me true peace and satisfaction. I believe that you died and rose again so that my sins could be forgiven. By faith, I place my trust in you and invite you to come in and take control of every area of my life. Thank you for forgiving my sin and for the gift of eternal life. From now on, I will trust you for peace of mind and direction in all areas of my life. I ask this in your name, Amen.

This gift that you've just received has many facets. You are now a part of God's loving family that offers you so much to enjoy. But, as in any relationship, it is vital to become better acquainted with your Heavenly Father and your new brothers and sisters in Christ. There's a church waiting for you with open doors. There's a Bible study group waiting for you with open arms.

THE UNWRAPPED GIFT

Have you ever received a gift that was so beautifully adorned you didn't want to unwrap it? You just wanted to admire it the way it was, hesitating to discover the treasure awaiting you inside.

Perhaps you've recognized your need and accepted God's gift of salvation through his son, Jesus, but haven't discovered all God has in store for you, not realizing God has a purpose for your life. The Bible tells us, "No mere man has ever seen, heard or even imagined what wonderful things God has ready for those who love the Lord" (1 Corinthians 2:9).

If you have become more aware that God is a very personal God and can be trusted with the smallest detail to the most monumental event you are facing, I encourage you to place your confidence in him. As a loving Father, he wants to be part of everything you do and is waiting to enfold you in his arms.

> Heavenly Father,
> Forgive me for failing to see how much you have wanted to become a vital part of my life on a day-to-day basis. Help me to entrust everything I have and everything I am to you. In Jesus's name, Amen

God bless you as you begin this exciting journey!

SHARE YOUR THOUGHTS

If you would like to share your thoughts or comments with Karen, please contact her at:

becomingawomanofpurpose@gmail.com.